658.85

Successful
Selling
in a week

CHRISTINE HARVEY

Hodder & Stoughton

A MEMBER OF THE HODDER HEADLINE GROUP

Also available:
Successful Selling in a Week Cassette – ISBN 0 340 65470 8

Order queries: please contact Bookpoint Ltd, 130 Milton Park,
Abingdon, Oxon OX14 4SB. Telephone: (44) 01235 827720, Fax:
(44) 01235 400454. Lines are open from 9.00 – 6.00, Monday to
Saturday, with a 24 hour message answering service. Email
address: orders@bookpoint.co.uk

British Library Cataloguing in Publication Data

Harvey, Christine
  Successful Selling in a Week. –
  (Successful Business in a Week Series)
  I. Title II. Series
  658.85

ISBN 0 340 70538 8

First published 1992
Second edition 1998
Impression number 10 9 8 7
Year   2003 2002 2001

Cover photo from Telegraph Photo Library

Typeset by Multiplex Techniques
Printed in Great Britain for Hodder & Stoughton Educational,
a division of Hodder Headline Plc, 338 Euston Road, London
NW1 3BH by Cox & Wyman Ltd, Reading.

■■■C O N T E N T S■■■

ABOUT THE AUTHOR

Christine Harvey is the best-selling author of five books published in 19 languages and 32 foreign editions. These include *Your Pursuit of Profit, Successful Motivation in a Week, Successful Selling in a Week, The Christine Harvey System of Public Speaking and Leadership Building* and *Secrets of the World's Top Sales Performers* which has sold over 150,000 copies.

As an international speaker and consultant, Christine Harvey has addressed audiences in 20 countries and the world's top companies including IBM, Sony, Arthur Andersen, Toyota, Russian Business School, Australia Institute of Management, British American Life Insurance, Dean Witter, the US Mortgage Brokers Association and Lloyds Merchant Bank.

As an award winning sales executive in her own right, she went on to found three companies. She has hosted, produced and appeared on television and radio shows in Europe, Asia, Australia and America. She has served as Chairman of the London Chamber of Commerce West Section and on a number of Boards worldwide.

Selling as an occupation is something that leaves most people terror-stricken. Yet selling is such an integral part of running any business that good sales people are in great demand.

Succcssful selling is *not* a 'fly by the seat of the pants' process. It is, in fact, a structured set of systems which all professional high achievers learn.

We shall look at each of these steps one day at a time. The seven steps to successful selling are:

- Plan your success
- Product and service knowledge
- Discover the buying motives
- Overcome objections and turn them to your advantage
- Presentations and closings
- Action-provoking systems
- Self-motivation and support systems

Successful selling brings with it high success, career progression, self-satisfaction and personal growth.

Plan your success

Do you remember the last time you changed jobs? Did it require a mental adjustment of your self-image? Chances are that you needed time to grow into the new shoes.

I remember sitting on a plane from London, bound for Chicago, to meet my first prospective client after I started my company. I still felt allegiance to my old company, my old job and my old colleagues because I had no experiences to draw upon for my new role. If you are just starting out in sales, or changing companies, you may experience this too.

However, psychologists say that we can do a lot for ourselves to speed up the acclimatisation process. If we visualise ourselves working in the new role, feeling comfortable in the new role and succeeding in the new role, we will acclimatise faster.

Whether we are new to sales or want to improve our returns, we'll be adopting new methods of operation. We'll be forcing ourselves in new directions, putting ourselves under new pressures, disciplining ourselves, setting new goals – all of these will require that we see ourselves differently. The sooner we do this, the sooner we'll succeed.

Let's look at the specific areas in which you'll want to see yourself operating successfully as preparation for selling:

Success preparation

- Set overall goal
- Break the goal into daily work segments
- Carry out these daily segments
- Gain prospective customers
- Spend time on critical activities
- Create self-management system charts
- Organise work systems

Set overall goal

Start at the top of the list and set your goals. What do you want to achieve? Calculate it in some specific terms. Will it be a monetary figure, a percentage or multiple of a target set by your company, a possession to be acquired, or even a promotion?

Now think about how to convert that goal to the actual number of sales you need in order to achieve your target. Good. Now the next step is critical and this is the step most unsuccessful salespeople avoid. Divide your total sales into weekly and daily sales and then calculate the work necessary to achieve that.

Calculate workload

- How many sales do I want? ....
- How many prospects will I need to see in order to make one sale? ....
- How many prospects do I need in order to reach my total sales target? ....
- How many activities do I need to do to generate one prospect?
  — Telephone calls ....
  — Direct mail letters ....
  — Exhibitions or seminars ....
  — Advertisements ....
  — Cold calling ....
  — Other...
- What daily activity schedule and results do I have to maintain in order to achieve my goal? (Include visits, telephone calls and all of the above.)

....
....
....
....
....
....

Self-deception

Bob Broadley, one of the world's top insurance salesmen, puts it in strong terms. He says that the single biggest failure salespeople make is *self-deception.* He said he wasn't 'born with success'. He had to study the most successful sales people he could find.

His advice? 'Don't fool yourself into thinking you're selling when you're not in front of the right number of people every day. Working eight hours per day is not the point. It's what you do in those eight hours that counts.'

If you're not in front of enough prospects, you won't sell enough to make your target. And how do you get in front of enough prospects? By making enough appointments. It's that straightforward. 'Yet many people fool themselves thinking they are selling when in fact they are doing busy work,' says Bob.

Remember, the difference between success and failure often is neglecting to break down the overall target into daily targets and tasks.

Let's look at advice from people who succeed year after year. How do they put this principle into practice?

One salesman with a world wide reputation for success is Ove Sjögren from Electrolux in Sweden. He has calculated his yearly target and broken it down in to a daily figure. He knows exactly how many sales he must make per day. He knows how many prospects he must see each day.

He stresses that staying at the top is easy if you know how much you must do every day and you do it.

Not me!
'Oh, daily targets don't relate to me,' many people argue. That's the biggest misconception I hear from seminar delegates. They really believe they can't break *their* activity into daily targets.

This is the first mental change we must *all* make if we are to succeed in selling. Sales come about from methodically carrying out the right practices, day in and day out.

Whether we sell large systems to governments which require three years to close, or retail products to customers which take three minutes to close, we still have to calculate *which* daily component parts will lead us to success. Even if we only want three customers per year, we'll have to be negotiating with six, nine or twelve prospects constantly. We need to know *how many* and keep this running *constantly*.

In the research undertaken for my book, *Secrets of the World's Top Sales Performers*, I found that every single top sales performer in every industry knows their daily sales target and daily activity schedule. Did their companies tell them? No. They've calculated it themselves. It's exactly what we all must do if we want true and lasting success.

You must know your daily targets for finding prospects and do that first. That means making appointments and seeing prospects. All else is secondary.

Create daily segments

Why do we put so much stress on daily sales targets and daily activity targets? It's because we've seen so many failures by talented, hard-working, well-meaning people who deserved to succeed. No one ever sat them down and said, 'Look, success comes by doing the right number of activities day in and day out'.

Make reminders

We know that you are reading this book in order to succeed. You want to use a strategic approach. You want to avoid the pitfalls of others. Therefore, take today to plan your targets. Plan your systems for reaching your targets. Draw up wall charts, pocket memos – anything and everything you need to remind yourself that hard work alone will not bring you success. It's a matter of scheduling and seeing the right number of people today as well as carrying out specific activities which will allow you to see the right number of people tomorrow.

Calculate

What is the right number? If we need one sale per day and we have to see three prospects in order to convert one to a sale, then we need three sales visits per day. That's if we can do one-call closings; in other words, we only need to see each prospect once. But what if we need to see each prospect twice on average and we need to make one sale per day? How many sales visits will we need to do every day? Six.

1 sale × 3 prospects × 2 visits = 6 visits per day

We'll need time for making appointments, and following up on promises we make during the appointments. Therefore, the need for planning our targets and breaking them into daily workloads is essential.

Is 'our best' a measure?

What if you didn't do the calculation? What if you just worked as hard as you could? What do you think the result would be?

Perhaps this example will help. On one of my speaking engagements in Singapore, a journalist approached me and asked, 'Why do you so often stress the importance of daily targets? Isn't it enough for people to just do their best?'.

'Look at it this way,' I suggested. 'What if you were training to be an Olympic champion runner? Would you go out every day and practise running any distance at any speed, just doing your best? Or would you know exactly how far you had to run and at what speed you had to run in order to meet your defined goal?'

'Oh yes, I see,' she responded. It seemed to click for her. It's painful for people to work hard and do their best, to have high expectations and then be let down. However, with daily targets set, you are able to work sharp and with purpose. You won't fail by thinking sales will come to you magically, suddenly or later.

Pitfalls for business owners too
New business owners have exactly the same problem, and we can learn from them. Here's an example. Two very talented young dress designers with their own shop asked advice for succeeding in their business. They had a lot of loyal customers, but they were afraid they wouldn't make enough money to stay in business.

Here are the questions which need answers:

- How much money do we need to make?
- What are our expenses?
- How many do we need to sell per year to cover all our expenses and leave us with a profit?
- How many is that per week?
- What do we need to do in order to sell that many each week?

They hadn't thought about it that way. They were just going to do the best they could. Were they unusual? No. That's the naïve approach you want to avoid regardless of your industry.

Are 'good products' enough?
I was very fortunate to work with a British enterprise agency launched by Prince Charles which helps people start up new businesses. Through that experience of working on the Board, I saw hundreds of people who thought it was enough to have a 'good product' and 'do their best.' Yet as time went on, those who succeeded learned that they had to know *exactly* what their sales targets were every week and every day. Then they had to focus all their energy on making sure those targets were met, to ensure that they didn't go out of business.

You don't want to be out of business; that is, out of the sales business. There are tremendous opportunities in sales: opportunities for self-development, opportunities for promotion, opportunities for helping people, job satisfaction, financial wealth and even progression towards running your own business if that's what you want. Yet, few business owners today succeed without strong emphasis and skills on the sales side. And likewise, few people today in the corporate world progress without being able to sell their ideas.

Millions of people are involved in the production of products or services. All of their jobs rely on people being able to sell those products or services. Corporations need you. The economies of the world rely on continued sales. Your skills and your success are more important than you realise.

Measure your results

Whatever your goal, start now by measuring your targets and breaking them into daily targets and tasks. Remember that today is your day of preparation and your success later will mainly depend on your plan and your dedication to your plan .

Two aspects on this chart are the most critical to measure. These are:

- Number of sales visits (target and actual)
- Number of sales (target and actual)

Self-management wall chart

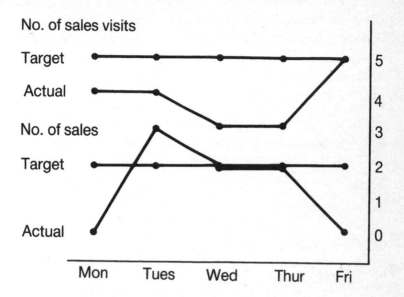

If you are really determined to succeed, you'll also to chart the following:

Self-management systems

- The number of telephone calls you make for appointments (target and actual)
- The number of direct mail letters you send (target and actual)
- The number of referral leads you get from customers before and after the sale (target and actual)
- Any other methods you use for finding prospective customers

These will become your self-management systems.

Predicting shortfalls
If your wall chart shows you that your actual sales visits are 25% below your target for one week, you can expect to be 25% down on sales unless you make up that number of visits next week.

Sales do not come about magically, and that's what your management control wall charts remind you of so graphically and unmistakably.

Mental readiness

Will you reach the success level you hope for?

Much of your success will depend on coming to terms with the actual component parts of salesmanship.

Selling is not a mystical process. It's a predictable, logical, step-by-step process like a production line. When we put in the right component parts, we get the correct end-product. When we put in fewer component parts than necessary, we get an inferior end-product. There is no mystery about salesmanship.

Planning our success by setting our daily workload is the first component part. The next six chapters give the other component parts. When we carry out each component part in the right quantity, with the right quality and frequency, we have success.

Our results come from our actions, not from our understanding. It's said that, 'Knowledge without action serves no one'. This is never more true than in sales. Pick up your pen and start now to create your targets *and* your self-management system charts. Success is in your hands.

> Remember, knowledge without action serves no one.

Gaining product and service expertise

The purpose of this chapter is to help you create a personal plan for developing expertise in product and service knowledge which will help you reach the top of your profession.

How much expertise?

Let's start at the beginning. How much knowledge do you need? Perhaps this idea will help you. Dale Carnegie advised his students of public speaking, 'Learn 40 times as much as you will use'.

Why 40 times? It's because our store of information is like a fully charged battery. It shows in our enthusiasm, our self-confidence and most of all in our *competence*. Certainly that's true of selling too.

Let's stop for a moment and think of our customers. How do they view us? Aren't we the only link between the manufactured product or service and themselves? They have to rely on us to tell them *each and every thing* that they might need to know.

It makes sense, then, to have a 40-fold store of knowledge in reserve for every eventuality, over and above what we might use in a single sales discussion with a single customer. Therefore, we need to focus on getting as much knowledge as we can, as quickly as possible.

Who is responsible?
First, let's set the ground rules and clear any misconceptions. In order to reach the top with the desired level of expertise, we should consider these two principles:

- Expect to invest in ourselves
- Don't expect the company to provide all of our training

Invest in yourself
How many years do doctors, lawyers or accountants spend in preparing themselves for their profession? If we want to become experts, the first realisation we must make is that we must invest in ourselves. We have to develop our own plan. If our company trains us, fine. But we cannot use the lack of training as an excuse to hold us back. Success is in our own hands.

Finding sources of knowledge

Where do we start? We want to set a schedule for absorbing our 40-fold expertise in the shortest possible time. Let's look at some effective options.

Sources of product expertise

- Interview current customers
- Study product literature
- Study service literature
- Study operations manuals
- Take technicians on sales visits
- Accompany other sales professionals on sales visits
- Have discussions
  - with operations people
  - with managers
  - with product development people
  - with distributors
- Observe the production line
- Observe field service
- Take training courses of all kinds

Interview current customers

Interviewing current customers is one of the most valuable yet least exploited options for salespeople. Customers give us the information from the *user's* point of view, which is invaluable.

Gain benefits

The customer doesn't want to know that the fax machine has 'group 3, high speed, digital transmission technology'. They only want to know that their document can reach their colleague in Australia in 28 seconds *because* of this group 3, high speed technology.

We must always stress the benefit using the technology as proof that the benefit exists.

Why else are we so bullish on visiting or talking to current customers? Because they are a bottomless pit of testimonials, references, new business, add-on business, referrals, inspiration, enthusiasm, and information about competitors. Moreover, they can supply quotable stories, even material for press releases and feature stories. But the most important part is your instant education.

Here is an example. Some years ago I was involved in selling a computer service. Because all of us on the sales-team were hired from industry and knew little about computers, we each needed to get our own training as quickly as possible. I therefore arranged to accompany a technician on a trouble-shooting call and after she sorted out the problem, I asked the client a question. 'What made you choose our system over the competitor's?'

'It's so fast to use and error free,' he said. 'We previously agonised over errors in our systems. Now we complete input forms every morning. It takes half an hour maximum. Then the results come back – perfect, no aggravation,' he said.

That was a testimonial I could use to emphasise speed and accuracy. It gave our sales team a valuable reference letter and later we turned it into a press release which gave it added value.

So you can see that the benefits of interviews with current customers are endless. Through interviews we gain confidence in our product and company. We learn the benefits to the user. We build a rapport which can later lead to further business. We acquire testimonial stories about how the service is used. We gain confidence and inspiration.

We can then repeat the process with different industry group users until we have the knowledge we need. The time it takes you will be well worth your while.

Plan your strategy

Use today to plan your strategy for building your product/ service expertise. The checklist below will help you decide which methods to apply. Who will you go to in order to get the information? How long will you allocate to each method? When will you do it? Use the list opposite to create your action strategy.

Set up your system today. You may want to call one or two current customers to set up appointments for interviews. Or you may even want to have the discussion by telephone today if appropriate. Naturally, it's always better to do it in person if possible. Distances, time and products will dictate the appropriate approach.

Look again at your strategy. Have you allocated enough time?

Product/service expertise

Method	Yes/No	Who	How long	When
• Interview current customers	---------	-----	-------------	-------
• Study product literature	---------	-----	-------------	-------
• Study service literature	---------	-----	-------------	-------
• Study operations manuals	---------	-----	-------------	-------
• Take technicians on sales visits	---------	-----	-------------	-------
• Accompany other sales professionals on sales visits	---------	-----	-------------	-------
• Have discussions				
– with operations people	---------	-----	-------------	-------
– with managers	---------	-----	-------------	-------
– with product development people	---------	-----	-------------	-------
– with distributors	---------	-----	-------------	-------
• Observe the production line	---------	-----	-------------	-------
• Observe field service	---------	-----	-------------	-------
• Take training courses	---------	-----	-------------	-------

You may want to spend an hour a day next week reading technical literature or perhaps two hours today. You may want to invite a technical person to accompany you on your next sales visit, or arrange to accompany them on a technical visit. Decide now and allocate time in your diary.

Attend training courses

You may want to persuade your manager that he or she should fund a training course for you from their budget. If you do, you should be prepared to 'sell' your idea, explain the benefits the company will get from your enhanced skills. Remember, your boss may have to sell the idea up the line.

But beware of the bottom line; that is, your commitment to your own training. If the answer is no, you may have to invest in yourself. Be prepared to take responsibility for your own success.

Professionals spend time and money preparing for success in their career, and selling is as demanding and challenging as any career.

What steps can you take to find training courses which will be valuable to you?

Learn at every appointment

One top sales manager I knew summed it up well when he advised, 'The day you stop learning in sales is the day your professionalism dies'.

After every sales call with any of his sales-staff, whether they were new to sales or experienced, he always said, 'Tell me two new things you learned from that visit'. That's good advice for all of us.

Implement your strategy

Take time now to look back over the options for developing product and service expertise. Decide which options are right for you. Then draw up a segmented strategy of how much time to devote to each option. Take today to plan those segments.

Remember, the day you stop learning is the day your professionalism dies.

Discover the buying motives

One university professor I know shocks his class by saying, 'No one makes any decision in life that doesn't benefit himself in some way'.

The students always protest, 'Surely that's not true. People often do things for humanitarian reasons. There are church groups. There are people who do things unselfishly'.

'Yes,' the professor counters, 'that's true. But let's look under the surface. What motivates them? What makes them take their decision? What do *they* get out of it?'

Then he goes on to explain that even in humanitarian actions, people feel good about themselves and their noble actions. This is a benefit to them.

Motives can be psychological
Gradually the students learn to examine the motives behind decisions and to look for what drives people. They discover that the benefits people get can be psychological as well as material.

Think of this as it relates to your own sales situation. What benefits do your customers get? Don't think about what the product does. Think about the benefit to the buyer.

The correct way to find motives

Perhaps you've heard this saying. 'The person who asks the questions is in control of the meeting.'

In order to be in control of your success, it's necessary to ask questions. Not just any questions. They must be questions that lead to the customer's needs and buying motives.

One time I sat with a new employee and discussed a prospective client. I told the employee that it would be his job at the upcoming meeting to ask questions that would lead us to the buying motive of the client. He said he could do it because he considered himself to be a good conversationalist.

After 45 minutes with the customer it was obvious that my employee was taking the conversation in all directions *except* to discover why he might want our service. The employee hadn't learned to *target* his conversation in a certain direction. It was a hit and miss approach.

Hit and miss doesn't work in selling because we don't have the time we have in social relationships. We have to ask precise questions that lead us in the direction of the answers we need in order to identify our clients' needs, and then stress the corresponding benefits.

Such questions could be:
- *'What would you be expecting from a supplier?'*
- *'What benefit would you be hoping for?'*
- *'What one thing could we offer to convince you to change suppliers?'*

Those are three precise and very directive questions. They lead you in the direction of finding out the needs and motives of your client. Now think of more questions. Create your own list.

Think of yourself as a yachtsman with the rudder of your sailboat in the grip of your hand. As your boat goes slightly off-course, you move the rudder to bring it back on-course.

To become a powerful and directive questioner we need only think of ourselves as yachtsmen. When the conversation starts to go off-course, when it starts to wander aimlessly in this direction or that, we need to bring it back on course. 'Yes, I see what you mean. That's important to know. I remember you said earlier that you wanted a high clarity screen . . . ,' and so we are back on track. 'What benefits would you be looking for – higher productivity, faster turn-round, less frustration?' we continue.

Practise, practise, practise bringing the conversation back to ascertaining the customer's needs and motives. The person who asks the questions sets the direction. We must make sure we know what direction we want to go in.

Get the logical and psychological motives
We can actually help our buyer on two levels: the logical level and the psychological level.

Another way to look at this is to say that every corporate purchase has a benefit to the corporation and a benefit to the individual. Most salespeople focus only on the logical or corporate benefit. Yet the psychological or individual benefit can be, and often is, far more powerful and persuasive.

Why not go away to a quiet place and list your prospects. What are their emotional or individual buying motives?

- *What do they need and want?*
- *What benefits can I match to their needs?*

Check your assumptions

The title of this chapter is '*Discover* the buying motives'. Yet sales are lost because people *assume* they know what the customer wants.

Checklist of assumptions about needs and buying motives

List the assumptions you and your colleagues may be making about the needs and buying motives of your prospects:

- Price (too high). Why?
- Price (too low). Why?
- Extras (important). Why?
- Extras (not important). Why?
- Distance
- Delivery time
- Features
- Benefits
- Service

List all the assumptions you can think of. Examine them and ask why you have this assumption. Is it something this customer said? Is it something ingrained from the last customer? Is it something your colleague said about the customer? Does it need to be validated?

The best method of checking our assumptions is to call our customers and ask if our assumptions are right. Then we must *listen* to their answers and reshape our presentation or proposal accordingly. If it's a team-sell, we need to convince our colleagues to avoid these costly assumptions also.

Thus we realise how much time and effort we've lost barking up the wrong tree, and change our approach to selling. If you really want to excel in avoiding assumptions, track the reasons for every sale you lose or have lost. The best companies do just that.

In *Secrets of the World's Top Sales Performers*, Sony employees told us that they sit together and examine their approach and assumptions. They don't point fingers in order to place the blame outside; rather they decide what caused the loss and how to overcome it next time.

During your analyses, you'll discover that your assumptions on buying motives are fatal. It's a fast cure and a lesson every professional needs to learn .

Decision makers' assumptions to avoid
When calling to find out why the business was lost, you'll discover that there were pressures within the organisation that eluded you.

One seminar delegate we had, told the story of working closely for several months with the managing director of a company to identify his needs. He thought everything was perfect until he presented the final proposal and discovered that the production director also had influence.

What did he do wrong? His error is common and painful. He assumed that the MD's authority was enough. He didn't identify the people who influenced the purchase decision and therefore didn't find out their needs.

The time to present motives

One computer systems saleswoman in America is constantly ranked at the top of her national sales team. Janet achieves 190% of her target year after year.

Let's look at the critical difference between Janet's approach, which keeps her at the top end, and the approach of salespeople average in performance.

She has an invaluable two-tier approach. She visits the prospective client on a fact-finding mission, and interviews them thoroughly to ascertain their needs and motives. She also makes sure she interviews everyone who influences the buying decision.

Only then does she present the benefit of her product and in such a way that it precisely meets the customer's needs.

She focuses all her energy and all her words on what the customer will gain from the system. Her preparation time goes into thinking about how the system can match the needs of each individual and therefore justify the costs in their minds.

The average sales person doesn't hit the bull's eye because their questionning process fails them. Their needs analysis and motive analysis are missing or inadequate. They do not sell as often as they could. Let's look at the vital rules:

- Never assume you know the customer's needs and motives
- Identify all individuals who influence the purchase decision
- Interview to uncover needs and motives
- Get their logical and psychological motives
- Go away and think
- Express the product or service benefits that match the customer's needs and motives
- Only then present to the customer with complete focus on *their* buying motives

Present motives linked to benefits

During your 'think' before your presentation, you will have
made notes, listed those who influence the decision, thought
about everyone's needs. You will have looked at the
presentation from all sides, like a three dimensional picture.
You'll have thought about all angles in preparation for your
next approach to them.

You might want to put it all on a grid.

Our Product Benefits	A	B	C	D	etc.
Needs of Company X					
1.					
2.					
3.					
Needs of Company Y					
1.					
2.					
3.					
Psychological needs Customer A					
1.					
2.					
3.					
Psychological needs Customer B					
1.					
2.					
3.					

Ready, steady, go

Armed with our list of buying motives and the benefits we can offer to meet their needs, we have nothing to fear.

Now we see clearly what to present. When we go to our customer, we will not be 'winging it'. We will not be improvising. We will be presenting our product or service in such a way that they can see the benefit and justify it. Their logical and emotional needs will be met. It will all fall into place .

Why? Because the customer's buying motive has had the pre-eminent position. You will have stepped into the customer's shoes and seen it from their point of view. You will be on their side of the fence and they will feel it.

> Remember, the person who asks the
> questions guides the direction.
> Make sure you steer in the direction of the
> buying motives.

Overcome objections

When we are handling objections, whether in selling or in everyday life, we're dealing with very human factors. We're dealing with people's need to be heard – people's need to be recognised for their opinions, fears, doubts and misunderstandings.

This takes finesse on our part. It takes time to stop and think. It takes determination to do things a new way.

Let's look at two examples in which we can apply the objections process to improve our results. Some years ago I gave a speech to 150 people from a political party which had previously taken our sales and marketing course.

After my speech I asked some of them, 'What did you implement from the course so far?'. Their immediate answer was, 'Better ways of handling the objections of our electorate'. Thus we see the importance of being able to sell and defend our ideas. The same is true in the workplace and in all areas of life.

Here is a personal example of the power of the objection process. After learning this process, one of our instructors reported that he had tremendously improved his relationship with his teenage daughter. 'How did it happen?' I asked. 'I applied the three-part objection technique we teach in class,' he reported. His daughter told him that it was the first time she felt he had really listened to her. Thus her attitude and co-operation improved enormously.

In selling, if we don't clear the objection, it lingers like smoke in the mind of our customers. We must clear it just as we clear smoke from a room. Think of a large fan blowing the smoke out through an open window. That's what you're doing with the objection clearing process.

The process

The three-part process can have extraordinary results for you too. The steps are:

* The prelude (psychological)
* The explanation (logical)
* The clarification question (psychological)

The prelude
Our prelude segment prepares people to listen by melting down their defences.

Most people put the spotlight on to the explanation. They forget that the explanation falls on deaf ears if we don't break down the defences of the customer first. When I refer to the 'customer' in this case, of course I'm referring to our

listener, be it our boss, our spouse, our child, our political
constituents, our colleague or our client.

If the customer says no, then we have to start again with the
prelude segment. But the chances are that he won't, because
our words have made him feel that we understand his
concerns. We didn't ride roughshod over his objections. We
took time to sympathise, to line up on his side, to see his
point of view first, before we brought out our logical
explanation.

The prelude gives the other person a chance:

- To cool down
- To realise we're on his side
- To feel understood
- To have his concerns validated
- To save face
- To build a rapport with us

Do you think those points are important to the person with the objection? Of course they are. That's why it improved our instructor's relationship with his daughter, in the example above. She felt as though her father had taken time to listen to her and care about her point of view .

What people want from us
We need to think about this point carefully. Isn't that what every person wants from us – to be listened to and to have their concerns recognised? And isn't that what's missing when we bypass the prelude segment and go straight to our explanation segment?

Don't make that mistake. If you do, you'll just be handling objections the old way and you'll have no improvement.

The key point to understand here is this: No matter how good your explanation segment, it won't sink in until you convince people that you sympathise with and value their concerns.

Handling price objections

Let's look at a hot subject with salespeople – overcoming the price objection. First let's look at the difference between success and failure. The truth is that most ineffective salespeople *think* that they could sell *if* their price was lower.

Yet, most top salespeople don't consider price to be an obstacle. Why? Think about this because chances are that you've fallen into the same trap from time to time.

Why do the top performers breeze past the price objections when others are blocked?

The reasons are *attitude* and *understanding.* If we think our price is too high, you can be sure we'll transmit that to our customer. If we think our price is too high, we won't look for the benefits which justify the price.

Would our companies really stay in business if the price didn't justify the benefits? Probably not.

If the price really is too high, then it's time to cure the problem or change jobs. The point is this: *don't* make the mistake of the majority of ineffective sales people which is to try and ignore price justifications.

We must get out there and *learn* price justifications as the top performers do. That will form our logical explanation segment. And we must remember to prelude our price justification.

Why not put the technique in to practice and see what you can achieve? I think you'll be surprised. You can work on your answers today by using the chart on p. 50 and the example which follows.

Example
'I like your product, but the price is too high,' our customer says. At this point we don't know what he means by 'too high'. Higher than the competition for exactly the same thing, higher than his budget, higher than his expectation? But we can't ask yet because we haven't broken down the resistance.

The prelude
Think about what your prelude should be. It must be right for you and your customer. Fill the appropriate response into the chart on p. 50, perhaps something like this:

'Yes, I can understand your concern about price, Miss Whitehill. With the economy the way it is, businesses have to make every penny count. In fact, you're not alone. A lot of our clients told us they were worried about price before they used our service. Yet afterward they come back and tell us they had a 100% payback within three weeks.'

The explanation
Now we're making our transition to the logical explanation. In our prelude we sympathised with *the customer's* concern. We even said others felt the same.

We're going out of our way to prove we understand the concern from the customer's point of view.

Now, what *are* our price justification benefits? What reasons do we have that will justify the expenditure? Chances are that you'll find dozens when you start digging.

You'll be most effective if you get these from current and past customers, because you'll have high credibility stories to tell your clients.

For example, 'Mr Phillips at Tarmaco told me last week that they reduced their down time by 30 minutes per day with our service. This amounted to £10,000 per year.'

We should always match the customer's buying motives to the benefits we put forward. We won't talk about down time if it's irrelevant. We'll choose some benefit which does justify the price to that particular customer.

Brainstorm price justification
Look again at the objection chart on p.50 and list all the price justifications you can think of, then talk to colleagues and customers to expand the list.

Don't give up in despair. Remember, your preparation today will win you great rewards tomorrow. If you can't justify the price, your customer certainly can't. And you do want to be in the top ranks, don't you? That's why you're reading this book. It might seem like a daunting task, but once it's over it will be a gold mine at your disposal.

Start your list now before you read on. Even if it's just one or two points scribbled on a scrap of paper, it will get you started. The first step is the hardest and we want to get you on the winning path.

Remember, success is in our actions, not our realisations. We must be unrelenting with ourselves when we're forming new habits of success.

Clarification question

Now it's time for our clarification question. 'Have I satisfied your concerns on the price, Miss Whitehill?'

'Well, yes but I'm still concerned about the set-up cost,' she responds.

Good. Now we realise she's satisfied about the running costs, but she has a concern about the set-up costs. That's not a problem.

We use the three-part process again.

- We start at the beginning with another prelude.
- Then we go to the second step, the logical explanation. We give the benefits she'll receive in exchange for the price she pays for set-up.
- Then we go to the third step. Ask a question to see if she accepts our explanation.

Three-part objection process chart

1.) Prelude (human/psychological factor)
This opens the iron gate and breaks down the resistance.

2.) Explanation (logical factor)
Justification – benefits received in exchange for money paid out.

a.

b.

c.

d.

3.) Clarification Question (human/psychological factor)
Does our customer understand and accept our explanation?

Closing despite objections

We may never satisfy every concern a customer has. There will always be a competitor who offers something we don't offer. There will always be requests we can't fulfil. But when we can satisfy enough concerns to outweigh the doubts, we will succeed.

You can always use the direct approach: 'Miss Whitehill, we've discussed a checklist of ten requirements you hoped to meet. We couldn't meet two, but we *could* meet eight. I hope that the ones we can meet are the significant ones. I see those eight as being . . . .' (We list the benefits and price justifications which relate to her.)

We ask, 'Does it sound like the kind of service you would benefit from?' *Thus you help the customer put the situation into perspective.* Chances are that eight out of ten of the requirements are enough to meet their demands, especially if the requirements you can offer outweigh the ones you can't offer.

Be armed ahead

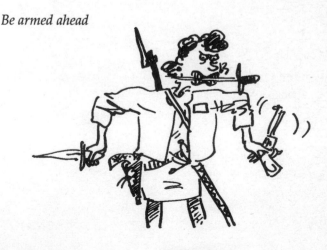

In preparation for your success ahead, you'll want to be armed with a list of likely objections and responses. Use the following chart and add as many sheets as you need to be prepared for most eventualities.

The answers which you prepare ahead on this chart can be used during sales presentations, telephone calls with prospective customers, and even in written communication.

Think now about all the areas in which you can use the three-part objection clearing process. Set a target today for improving your success rate in overcoming objections.

Now think of ways to:

- Practise it
- Remember to do it

Remember, the prelude is the key to having
your explanation accepted.
It breaks down the iron gate of resistance.

Objection reference chart

I. **Price**
   Prelude statement
   Explanation statement
   Satisfaction/question

2. **Delivery Time**
   Prelude statement
   Explanation statement
   Satisfaction/question

3. **Lack of expertise**
   Prelude statement
   Explanation statement
   Satisfaction/question

List any other likely objections:

4. ....
   Prelude statement
   Explanation statement
   Satisfaction/question

5. ....
   Prelude statement
   Explanation statement
   Satisfaction/question

6. ....
   Prelude statement
   Explanation statement
   Satisfaction/question

Presentations and closings

ASK – Customer's corporate buying motive
ASK – Customer's personal buying motive
KNOW – Product expertise
KNOW – Competition's strength and weakness
TELL – Links between needs and benefits
TELL – How you overcome objections
REVIEW – Needs and benefits
ASK – For their decision

Imagine each part of the presentation process as a separate waggon on a freight train. Each waggon is splendidly painted and inside it is filled with jewels.

Imagine that we are the railway inspectors. We walk along the side of the waggons together, sliding open the doors, and we see that each is filled with precious blue, yellow and green jewels.

These jewels represent:

* Facts
* Answers
* Links

The blue jewels represent the facts. The yellow jewels represent the answers we get. The green jewels represent the links between them.

In your sales presentation, when you combine the facts with the answers to your questions, you'll be able to make critical links. These links will be the green light to your sale.

Ask – the customer's corporate buying motive

Let's have a look inside the first waggon which is reserved for the customer's corporate buying motive. It will be almost empty when we first slide the door open. There will be a few facts here about why *most* people buy your product or service, but no specific facts about why *this* customer wants your product.

Assumptions don't count in sales. But as we ask questions, our waggon will fill with more and more facts, more and more precious jewels to help us link the buying motive to the benefits we have to offer.

The difference between you, a top sales performer, and a mediocre sales performer is that you will ask and ask and ask until your waggon is *filled* with facts and answers.

You'll find out the buying motives of every decision maker and every decision influencer. Each answer, each fact, will add another authentic, precious jewel to your first waggon.

The mediocre sales performers will not take time to ask because they assume that this customer is like all the others.

These false assumptions will lead them to impure links. The benefits they offer to the client will therefore be right for other customers but not necessarily right for this customer. Their time will be spent in vain. We won't let this happen to us because we realise that the time spent here is the most valuable of all.

Ask – the customer's personal buying motive

Most ineffective salespeople don't even push the door to this waggon open to look inside for the personal buying motive. They assume that the first waggon, the corporate buying motive, is all important. Yes, of course, we can't sell without satisfying the first waggon, but we must not discount one important factor.

> How will we get our buyer to fight personally for the sale?

If our customer contact in the corporate ladder is not personally motivated, why should he or she bother? After all, they have a job to do. Our sales efforts are an intrusion in their busy schedule.

We must identify what's in it for them. Is it:

- Saving time?
- Improving prestige?
- Reducing chaos?
- Reducing stress?
- Improving morale?
- Being up to date?
- Career advancement?
- More free time?

What is it that can motivate them personally?

We have to *ask*. We have to fill our waggon with genuine jewels of answers and facts in order to create the genuine links necessary to sell.

Know – product expertise

As we're turning their situation around and around in our minds, the links are building up faster and faster. We have our product expertise, those are the blue jewels in our waggon – the facts about our product and service. Now we are pouring in the yellow jewels – the answers to all our questions about the customer's corporate and personal buying motives.

The yellow and blue jewels are merging together in our mind and there are green sparks radiating from it. Those are our links – the combination of needs and benefits which are the reasons people will buy.

Naturally *your* waggon is brimming with knowledge. You've painstakingly talked to current customers to find out why they use your products. You've found out what benefits they get. You've built up first-hand stories about these benefits. You *know* what you have to offer to prospective customers in every detail. You've consulted your literature and your internal experts. You *know*.

Know – the competition's strength and weakness

Don't be afraid when you look inside this waggon.

Knowledge is power. The more we know, the better position we will be in to defend the benefits *we* can offer.

Our competitor may have some marvellous features, but if those features are not important to our client, we can still sell our benefits and win. The important thing is to be informed about what the competition *does* offer.

Then we won't be taken by surprise. Then we'll have time to turn it around in our mind, to become comfortable with it in a matter of fact way, to accept it as a feature, but put it in perspective.

'Yes,' we can say to ourselves, 'they have this feature, we have that. Now let's see who needs what. Let's look at the combination of benefits. Let's look at the cost of their benefits, and of our benefits and find out who is willing to pay what for those benefits.'

Then, when a customer says that our competitor has feature A, we'll be able to say, 'Yes, how do you feel about that feature? There are many features in the marketplace today. We've created ours by researching what our users most wanted for the price, ease of use,' etc. We then help the customer put it in to perspective.

By helping them to re-evaluate it, they may see that it's not important at all. The last salesperson may have made them feel they couldn't live without this 'all-singing, all-dancing' feature. But you, through your thoroughness of asking about their buying motives, can help them reflect:

- Do they really need this?
- Is it really an advantage?
- Will they really use it or is there a down side?
- What will it cost the customer either financially or in terms of learning, time, energy?
- What will they have to give up in order to gain that?
- What are the start-up and continuation costs?
- What does your package of features and benefits have to offer over theirs?

Knowledge is power. Because our waggon is full of knowledge about the competitors, we're in a position of strength, not weakness. We have little to fear. We'll be able to make links which work for us *and* the client.

Tell – the links between their need and your benefits

This is the moment of truth. I mean that literally. If we have the truth in terms of the buyer's needs and motives, if we have all the true facts about what our products can do, then we'll be able to make these links which give the buyer the mental green light to buy.

Selling today is not a manipulative process. Selling is helping the customer *see* what we have to offer and how it meets *their* needs. Notice that there are two parts to this and the second part is the key to success.

- What *we* have to offer
- How it meets *their* needs

Many ineffective salespeople focus on only the first part. They don't stop to realise that a customer wouldn't want to buy from someone who says, '*We* can do this, *we* can do this, *we* can do this'.

Who is the most important person in the world? The customer, of course. Will he or she feel important or feel cared about with a salesperson who talks only about their product and what it can do? Of course not. It's the *link* that makes the sale.

And we can't make the link without asking the customer what they want, what benefit they see, what their objective is, how they will use it. We don't do it as an interrogation, but rather from a position of consultative concern, of really trying to help.

Don't make the mistake of the ineffective salesperson, doing only half the job. You'll get only half the results. Do the whole job – make the link. Tell them how it meets their needs. Do this and your sales will more than double. This is true in every industry from retail to aerospace, from products and services to politics and education. If we want to sell anything, even an idea, we have to make a *flawless* link to the needs of the customer and the benefits they will get.

Make a list now of benefits and the likely motives of several prospective customers you'll see. This process will help you to think on your feet when you see them.

For example:

Needs – benefit link chart

Customer X
Need: *Customer wants to reduce overheads in the department next year by £15,000.*
Benefit: *System saves 20% man hours over your current system.*
Link: *You'll be able to do without your two temporary members of staff, saving £30,000. This £30,000 in overhead reduction will pay for the system the first year as well as reduce your running costs by £15,000, which was your goal. From then on you continue to save every year.*

1. Customer B
Need
Benefit:
Link:

2. Customer C
Need:
Benefit:
Link:

3. Customer D
Need:
Benefit:
Link:

After this link-building expertise is developed, you'll be able to communicate it verbally or in writing or both, thus increasing your closing rate.

Tell – how you overcome objections

Remember that objections linger like smoke. *You* won't let your customer's objections linger because you'll use the three-part objection technique from Tuesday's chapter. You'll make them realise that you *do* sympathise, you *do* understand. Then you'll give the explanation, and then you check to see if their concern is satisfied.

The ineffective salespeople don't see this waggon as full of helpful jewels. They see it as full of serpents and demons. They want to keep it locked shut. They want to skirt around it, staying as far away from it as possible *at all times*.

They want to sweep any hint of objection under the rug, hoping naïvely that it will never resurface. Little do they know that it smoulders there while the customer's mind becomes locked into the idea that their objection is reality. The customer is mentally packing their briefcase to go home while the ineffective salesperson continues to talk – *unheard*.

Your waggon on the other hand, is filled with blue and yellow jewels, because you've studied the likely objections and solutions, you've asked questions to find out what the concerns are.

You have the facts and answers. Therefore, you counter their objections quickly and easily as if holding the hand of the customer and walking them through a maze.

Review – needs and benefits

This is the most rewarding because it reveals the big picture. It puts everything into perspective for the customer. We've discussed features, benefits, needs, motives and objections. Now we're ready for the big picture.

'You told me you wanted to achieve X, Y, and Z. Is this still the case?' we must ask. We're helping them refocus on their needs, cut out the extraneous, forget the glorified benefits offered by the competitors.

Next we say, 'We've looked at our ability to meet X,Y, and Z through these methods . . . ' We put our benefits succinctly.

We don't elaborate so long that the customer forgets what X,Y and Z are.

Instead, we keep our choice of words focused on what they get, not what we give. 'With this machine you can get your documents to your office in Australia in 28 seconds. This will help you meet your objective of speeding up your communication time in order to win contracts.'

We won't say, 'This machine gives you group 3, high speed, digital transmission technology'. That's about the machine, not the customer. In addition, it doesn't mention his objective at all!

Yet that's how most uninitiated salespeople handle their presentation. Not you, of course, because your waggon is filled with the links – the jewels you've created by combining the needs with your benefits. You've sifted through the important versus the unimportant benefits to the customer, and you stress the important ones.

Now you, approach the last waggon – the be-all and end-all – the most vital.

Ask – for their decision

Recent research has shown that four out of five buyers *expect* to be asked to buy and *wait* to be asked. They don't volunteer to buy because they expect us, as part of the selling process, to ask. They wait, and if it doesn't happen, the buying moment passes by.

Let's look at what causes the critical moment to pass. Several things could happen. A competitor could ask for the order and get it, the customer could lose interest, or they could divert their funds to another project.

Therefore, the ineffective salesperson who doesn't ask, loses.

But your approach is different. From the beginning you have been thorough.

You've been letting the customer know how your product or service can help them, thus building commitment each step of the way. Your approach has let them see themselves using and benefiting from the product. Now when you ask for their decision, it's almost a foregone conclusion.

The benefits are crystal clear and they *line up exactly* with the customer's expressed needs.

You've been a catalyst in their search for the answer. You've helped them make their way through the maze of the unknown. You've helped them see the answer. Now when you ask for their decision, it's not an abrupt surprise. It's not a pressured, stressful event.

It's a natural evolution and our customer expects the question:

- 'Will you be taking this, then?' we might ask at the retail counter
- 'Does this seem like the kind of service which would benefit you?' we might ask in the sale of services
- 'Are the advantages we offer more meaningful than the other suppliers' we might ask in system sales
- 'Will you be working with us, then?'
- 'What implementation dates should we establish?'

Stop now and make a list of closing questions which feel right for you. Then when you get to this stage of your presentation, you won't have fear. Instead you'll see your box car filled with jewels of preparation. You'll have question after question which you designed, which work for you, not someone else.

Look at the freight train diagram on the first page of this chapter again. Do you know the secret of success over others who fail?

Most ineffective salespeople have no freight train at all. They have a little bit of product knowledge. They ask no questions to ascertain needs (they assume they know). They make no links to needs. They talk about the product only. They avoid objections whenever possible. And they don't ask for the business.

Would you want to hire a person like that to work for your business? Probably not and yet many managers have no choice. They must hire people, find ways to train them, motivate them and then hope for results.

The case is different with you. You're building your own professionalism, which makes you a rare commodity like a needle in a haystack.

Keep it up. The rewards are coming your way.

Remember, four out of five customers
wait for us to ask for the order.
Don't just present. Present *and* ask for the business.

Action-provoking systems

Striking while the iron is hot is a critical issue.

If we follow up a direct mail letter by telephone two weeks after it's sent, our call will be one-fifth as effective as it would be if we called after three days.

Why? Because people forget 80% of what they hear and read after two days. If we call shortly after the letter is posted, it will be fresh in their minds. If we call after three weeks, it won't.

The same is true of following up your prospect for a decision. What's the point of following up too late – after our competitor goes in or after our customer's budget is diverted?

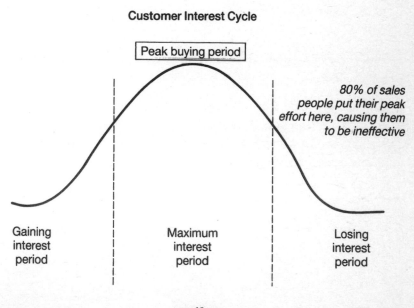

Customer Interest Cycle

Peak buying period

80% of sales people put their peak effort here, causing them to be ineffective

Gaining interest period

Maximum interest period

Losing interest period

Work hard or work sharp?
Yet the fact is that the majority of salespeople put their time and effort into the sales process too late.

Because they don't have action-provoking systems, they do things when they have time. Often this is too late.

Benefits of action-provoking systems
An action-provoking system will help you use your time where it counts – closing sales you have already started and starting the correct number of new prospects necessary to meet your targets.

What's your experience?
What kind of system do you have now?

Perhaps your experience is something like John's, an experienced salesman who came to our course. He was looking desperately for a way to increase his sales, but didn't know which way to turn.

We asked him what sort of action-provoking system he had and he said he wrote everything in his diary .

He said he carried everything over to the new page. Yet he admitted it was a lot of work to carry it forward and easy to miss or forget some. We looked at John's system and showed him this chart.

Action-provoking system

June	1	2	3	4	5	6	7	
1. *Smith & Co*	X							
2. *J Bloggs*								
3. *Estman*		X						
4. *Winters*		X						
5. *Peak and Co*								
6. *Johnston*								
7. *Withers*								
8. *Goodall & Co.*		X						
9. *Jones Bros*								
10. *Kent Air*								
11. *P.V. Anchor*	X							
12. *Bassett*		X						

'The beauty of this system,' we told him, 'is that we can walk into our office in the morning and see at a glance all our prime prospects. We know immediately which ones need action.

'On 1st June two companies need action from us. On 2nd June, four companies need action. They are the ones on lines 3, 4, 8 and 12. We just pull out those files and see what action is necessary.'

Two critical advantages
This system gives us two critical advantages. First, we're not likely to forget anyone. Their name is already entered. Secondly, we see at a glance much more about our prospect.

Let's say we call someone five days in a row and we miss them each time. We'll put an X down for the next consecutive day to remind us to call.

Later we'll have more critical information. We'll be able to glance at our sheet and see five X marks side by side. We'll know our efforts aren't succeeding. If this is a hot prospect, we'd better double up our efforts or take other action.

John looked sceptical but he went away and tried it. He called us a month later and said that the results of his new system put him up 40% on his sales figures after only 30 days.

Weakness of diary systems
'The diary system used to let me lose prospects too conveniently,' he told us. 'I've closed three sales this month by entering them into the master system. I know I would have turned the page and forgotten them in my old diary system. But because they were on the master sheet, I couldn't forget. It also made me more aware of my hard work on each prospect to date by seeing all my actions on one sheet. It made me more determined. I felt more in control.'

You may have the same reluctance that John had at first. You probably have a system that works for you. Fine. But the question is this:

- How well is it working?
- How much is slipping through the net that you're not aware of?

If you're looking for sales excellence, you have to turn over every stone of your present practices and see if there is a way of doing anything differently. You might find a way to make a small change in your practices which can get you enormously higher results.

Take today to examine your system and find the weak points or to develop a new system.

Computerised systems

Find the fallacy
'We have a perfect computerised system,' one salesman said. 'It tells us everything we've done for a prospect and what stage it's at.'

'Great,' we said. 'Does it tell you what day you have to take the next action? Does it show you on any given day a list of every prospect that needs action that day?'

'Well, I'm not sure,' he said. 'But we can pull up any prospect name and see the history of our actions.'

Think about what he's just said and see if you can find two fallacies. There's nothing wrong with history, but history is history. It doesn't provoke us to action on a certain day. What we're looking for is an action-*provoking* system, not historical record-keeping.

So there we have the first fallacy – confusing 'action taken' with action 'to be taken.' We want a report that lets us see a list of critical actions at the beginning of each day.

We also want a report that shows every company which should *have been* actioned in the past, with the number of days outstanding next to it like an aged debtors report which accountants use.

Only then do we have a good system. Only then do we know if we are striking while the 'iron is hot.'

Think again about the computer system of the salesman above and where you can see the second fallacy. When we asked him if he got a list of prospects that need action every day, he said he *wasn't sure.* What does that tell us about his use of the system? It tells us he wasn't using it, at least not to help him prompt his daily actions.

There's no point in having systems we don't use, and it becomes even more dangerous to think we have systems which help us when in fact they don't.

Look at your systems cold and hard now and ask, 'Are they really helping?'. If not, don't fool yourself into thinking they are. Make something quick and easy that works for you.

Manual systems for prospecting

Here's a useful manual system if you have hundreds of prospects to deal with at once.

This system consists of two ring binder notebooks. It's especially useful for telesales and telephone appointments.

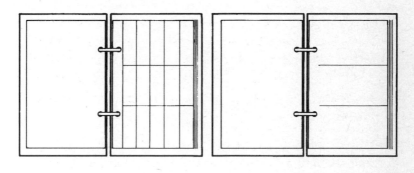

Action-provoking
ring binder 1

Prospect information
Ring Binder 2

In ring binder 1, we have 52 sheets, each representing one week of the year. On each sheet there is a week number, date, and days of the week across the top.

Down the side there is a place to list

- new prospects
- follow-up prospects
- appointment confirmations

Each sheet looks like the following:

Action-provoking Ring Binder 1				
Week Number				
Date				
New Prospects				
Mon	Tues	Wed	Thurs	Fri
Follow-up Prospects				
Appointment Confirmations				

On Monday, we walk into the office knowing that *we must activate a certain number of new prospects*. This number depends on our yearly target which we've broken down to a daily figure. Our prospects might come from a phone book or a Chamber of Commerce list, an industry list or a list of direct mail letters already posted.

Now we are ready to follow each up by telephone. We go to our second notebook which holds our prospect information.

Each sheet looks like this:

Prospect information ring binder 2	

Company Name   Code Number   *A- 103*
Person
Title
Address
Tel Number
Contact Date and Discussion Details

○

Company Name   Code Number   *A - 104*
Person
Title
Address
Tel Number
Contact Date and Discussion Details

○

Company Name   Code Number   *A- 105*
Person
Title
Address
Tel Number
Contact Date and Discussion Details

Three or more prospects can fit easily on one page. Because of the volume of prospects, we give each a code number which is easier to fit onto one sheet in the action-provoking ring binder.

By Monday night our sheet will look like this:

Action-provoking Ring Binder 1				
		Week Number_____ Date_____		
New Prospects				
Mon *A 105*	Tues *A105*	Wed	Thurs	Fri
~~A 106~~				
○ ~~A 107~~				
~~A 108~~				
A 109	*A109*			
~~A 110~~				
Follow-up Prospects				
~~A 63~~				
~~A 22~~				
○ ~~A 87~~				
A 88	*A 88*			
~~A 94~~				
Appointment Confirmations				
A 80	*A 80*			
~~A 26~~				
~~A 34~~				

You'll see that most prospects have been spoken to. These have diagonal lines through them. Prospects A105, 109, 88 and 80 have not been reached and therefore they are listed for action on Tuesday.

All records are kept in the prospect information ring binder A, and when that is full ring binder B is created.

Instead of using a series of notebooks for prospect information, file cards and file boxes can be used. But the notebook system prevents you from losing and misplacing cards and is much more convenient to transport from desk to desk or office to car.

When we get enough detail on one prospect, we may choose to start a file on them in the filing cabinet .

Take time to think of what system will work for you. Ask yourself:

- Where will I be when I use the system: car, desk, etc?
- How many entries will I need per day or week or month?
- What size book or record sheets do I need?
- Where will I store back-up info?
- What should the system look like?
- Who will use it: me, others?
- Who will enter the prospect names ?
- Who will enter the next actions required and the dates they must be done?
- What time of day will I take the actions, e.g. phone calls for appointments, phone calls for follow-up?
- Other questions to suit your situation

Without an action-provoking system, we don't have the support system we need. Our energy is fragmented and at the end of the month we're disappointed we didn't get the results we hoped for.

Take today to design an action-provoking system to make your efforts effective.

> Remember, your action-provoking system
> puts you in control

Self-motivation and support systems

'Everyone gets into the doldrums,' my first sales manager
told our sales team, 'but it's up to each of you to get
yourselves out of it.'

It would be nice if we all had sales managers who could
coach us and encourage us at every turn like the best
football coach.

But that's not practical. Managers are occupied with many
activities, and they can't possibly know our personality and
motivational needs as well as we can. And most
importantly, our success is reliant on whom – us or them?

Be your own coach
What's the message? We can't wait for someone else to
motivate us and set up our motivation systems for us. We
have to do it ourselves. We have to carry our own football
coach in our mind.

What support is needed?
Let's look at the kind of encouragement most sales people
need and want. Think about your own situation carefully.
What kind of support do you want when you have a 'down'
day? What kind of support do you want on normal days? Be
specific and complete the list for yourself.

- Goal setting
- Reaching a particular milestone
- Doing a mundane task consistently
- Cold calling
- Getting appointments
- Morale boost
- Confidence building

What motivation and support systems can you put into
place which will allow you to reach the top?

In this chapter we'll study the self-motivation and support
systems of the top achievers so that you can choose those
which would work for you and put the systems into place
today.

These success systems include:

- People
- Staying positive
- Eliminating doldrums
- Daring to be different
- Overcoming roadblocks
- Moving speedily towards your goal

People

What do you need from people? One top salesman talks to his wife from his car phone four times a day. He likes having someone to share his progress with, his ups and downs, his trials and tribulations.

Decide what support you want from people. All of us have people in our lives willing to support us, especially if we're willing to support them.

Who do you have? Open your mind to an expanded group of potential supporters. Partners, friends, co-workers, sales manager, other managers, people from your social groups, new age thinkers, the community, Chambers of Commerce, new acquaintances, customers.

Be specific about the kind of support you want from your list at the beginning of the chapter. Then set your goals, and share your progress with your supporter. Just reporting your progress to someone every day for a week, for example, can start you on a new path or help you form a new habit. I do this with a friend of mine who also owns a company.

Think now. Who can you talk to? You'll be surprised at how many people there are who would like to have this support reciprocated.

Staying positive

What are the chances that your customer will be positive if you aren't? The answer is zero.

We all have negative thoughts which pass through our minds, but it's our choice whether to hang on to them or not. The first step is to notice what our thoughts are.

Notice your thoughts
If you were to count the number of thoughts which flash through the mind in one minute, you would reach well over 60.

We can't hold onto every one, so why not pick the positive ones? So often in life we give in to the negative ones, forgetting that we are in charge of either holding onto or releasing those thoughts.

Release the negative
One top sales executive I interviewed for *Secrets of the World's Top Sales Performers* has developed his own mind-clearing process which is very effective.

He takes a walk after work reviewing how the day has gone, deciding what mistakes he's made, what to do about it and what to do differently next time. Then he releases any negative thoughts or guilt remaining about his mistakes.

In other words, he concentrates on correcting his mistakes rather than downgrading himself for making them in the first place.

Think now about what system you can put into place to:

- Listen to your thoughts
- Concentrate on correcting your mistakes
- Hang on to the positive
- Release the negative

Could you allocate time each day as this top achiever does? Could you write down the positive? What steps can you take? Think about it as you read the next paragraphs.

Eliminating doldrums

The best way to eliminate doldrums is to take a moment to acknowledge yourself. Take time to acknowledge what you do right. Take time to acknowledge your persistence, your stamina, your determination, your progress in being organised, your sales skill building, and so on.

Watch children as a clue to human development. A two-year-old says, 'I can do it, I can do it, I can do it.' A three-year-old says, 'I did it, I did it, I did it.' They go from conviction, determination and belief to success.

That's what we need to do too in creating success patterns. First, we have to have a positive attitude about the fact that we can do it, then we have to reinforce the fact that we have done it.

That's the reason you have to stop to give yourself acknowledgement for your progress and success. Don't wait until you reach the end result because you'll get into the doldrums waiting. Acknowledge yourself for the small steps along the way.

For maximum success, write down your success steps and review them every evening or when you're most likely to get the doldrums.

Most people find it easier to criticise themselves than to acknowledge themselves. It comes from years of practice. Now is the time to reverse the process. When you acknowledge yourself, your morale will go up. And high morale is essential to keep yourself going.

Why not make a list now of skills and qualities you can acknowledge in yourself. Then you'll be able to refer to these when you need a morale boost.

Skills and Qualities

_____	_____	_____
_____	_____	_____
_____	_____	_____
_____	_____	_____

Daring to be different

Another top sales executive hired a secretary after being in insurance only six months. No one else was willing to be so daring. But he saw the potential of doing what he did best and delegating everything else. Now he has four members on his support staff and *ten times* the average income.

Chances are that you're holding yourself back from something. It may be hiring a secretary or trying a new method no one else uses. It might be investing in equipment or support staff, or doing presentations or demos a different way. Whatever it is, look again. Think again. Don't be afraid to be different.

Perhaps you will be an inspiration, not only for yourself but for others. There are plenty of mediocre salespeople doing things in their standard way. If you want to be successful you have to be determined, committed, positive, disciplined and different.

Being different alone won't do it. But being different on top of being determined, committed, positive and disciplined can put you on a new plateau.

Think now. What are you holding yourself back from? Jot it down. Now decide what you are willing to do about it. Focus on the long-term effect you'll create, not the short-term resistance to change from those around you.

Think about the questions which follow.

> - What are you holding yourself back from? _____
> - What am I willing to do about it? _____
> - What result could I expect?_____

Overcoming roadblocks

Most people see a number of roadblocks between themselves and their goal. It looks something like this:

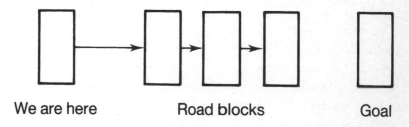

We are here   Road blocks   Goal

The mentality shift that helps us overcome roadblocks is as straightforward as this:

> Keep the goal in sight and focus determinedly on ways *around* the roadblocks

It looks like this:

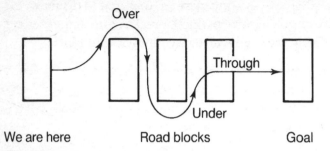

In reality, roadblocks are nothing more than challenges that help us grow. One person's roadblock is nothing to another person because they've already gained skills in that direction. So why not go in that direction to gain those skills as well?

Moving speedily towards your goal

Have you heard this important saying? 'Happiness is directly proportional to the speed you're moving toward your goal.'

Now, let's ask ourselves these questions:

- What happens if we have no goal?
- If our goal isn't very clear in our mind?
- If we see our goal as one big chunk rather than daily pieces?

All of those actions leave us feeling that we're moving slower or not at all towards our goal. We get caught in a downward spiral.

What can we do every day to make sure we're creating an upward spiral, moving closer to our goal? The answer is to have our goal clearly defined, break it into action segments, and tackle the segments every day without fail.

When you develop that discipline, success will be in your hands. Without it, you're giving your power away. What is *your* clearly defined goal? What are the segments which will help you reach it?

Take the most challenging path
One very successful woman I know says, 'When you come to a crossroad in life, take the most challenging path'. Why does she advocate this? Because challenges make us grow and make us feel good about ourselves. If we turn away from the challenging path, we stagnate.

I talked about this concept in a speech to a group of sales executives in Malaysia and among those attending was an IBM salesman. A year and a half later, he came to me and said that this advice had completely changed his life.

He had been doing well already, but with his new determination to take the most challenging paths at every turn, his life had become incredibly rich with new and exciting opportunities.

Think now of what challenging paths lie before you. Perhaps you haven't seen them in this light before. Perhaps they would also bring you rich, new and exciting opportunities.

It's important not to turn our back on them. Having the courage to take the challenging path and overcome the roadblocks requires conviction that we'll succeed. The best way to do this is to harness strength from past successes.

Think first of what roadblocks you perceive in front of you which stand in the way of your challenging path.

Consider your past successes
Think now of all your past successes. Think of your successes early in your career, early in your education. Think of any contest or competition you won, no matter how young you were. What quality did you have which helped you win? You still have it. Now is the time to harness this to help you overcome your roadblocks.

Every individual has a great deal more potential than they ever imagine. The goal or vision you have in your mind must be exactly right for you because no one else has that same vision. Don't let a simple roadblock stop you. Use your strengths to overcome it.

I'm behind you and I wish you success in your journey, every step of the way!

Christine Harvey
Intrinsic Marketing Administration Center
20 Station Road
West Drayton
Middlesex
UB7 7BY

Fax: 01895 422 565

> Remember, when you come to a crossroad
> in life,
> take the most challenging path

The week in summary

During the week, we have identified ways to master seven critical areas of selling. Here is a summary of the 'make or break' points of concentration:

Plan your success (Sunday)

- Set overall goal
- Create daily segments
- Measure your results

Gaining product expertise (Monday)

- Finding sources of knowledge
- Plan your strategy

Discover the buying motives (Tuesday)

- The correct way to find motives
- The time to present motives
- Present motives linked to benefits

Overcome objections (Wednesday)

- The process
- Handling price objections
- Closing despite objections

Presentations and closings (Thursday)

- Ask – customer's corporate buying motive
- Ask – customer's personal buying motive
- Know – product expertise
- Know – competition strength and weakness
- Tell – the links between their need and your benefits
- Tell – how you overcome objections
- Review – needs and benefits
- Ask – for their decision

Action-provoking systems (Friday)

- Computerised systems
- Manual systems for prospecting

Self-motivation and support systems (Saturday)

- Staying positive
- Daring to be different
- Overcoming roadblocks

Further *Successful Business in a Week* titles from Hodder & Stoughton and the Institute of Management all at £6.99

All Hodder & Stoughton books are available from your local bookshop or can be ordered direct from the publisher. Just tick the titles you want and fill in the form below. Prices and availability subject to change without notice.

To: Hodder & Stoughton Ltd, Cash Sales Department, Bookpoint, 39 Milton Park, Abingdon, Oxon, OX14 4TD. If you have a credit card you may order by telephone – 01235 400414.

E-mail address: orders@bookpoint.co.uk

Please enclose a cheque or postal order made payable to Bookpoint Ltd to the value of the cover price and allow the following for postage and packaging:

UK & BFPO: £1.00 for the first book, 50p for the second book and 30p for each additional book ordered up to a maximum charge of £3.00.

OVERSEAS & EIRE: £2.00 for the first book, £1.00 for the second book and 50p for each additional book.

Name: ....

Address: ....

....

If you would prefer to pay by credit card, please complete:

Please debit my Visa/Mastercard/Diner's Card/American Express (delete as appropriate) card no:

☐ ☐ ☐ ☐ ☐ ☐ ☐ ☐ ☐ ☐ ☐ ☐ ☐ ☐ ☐ ☐ ☐ ☐

Signature .... Expiry Date ....

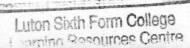